CONTEMPORARY LIVES

LEBRON JAMES

CHAMPION BASKETBALL STAR

ABDO
Publishing Company

LEBRON JAMES

CHAMPION BASKETBALL STAR

by Valerie Bodden

CREDITS

Published by ABDO Publishing Company, PO Box 398166, Minneapolis, MN 55439. Copyright © 2014 by Abdo Consulting Group, Inc. International copyrights reserved in all countries. No part of this book may be reproduced in any form without written permission from the publisher. The Essential Library™ is a trademark and logo of ABDO Publishing Company.

Printed in the United States of America,
North Mankato, Minnesota
102013
012014

Editor: Angela Wiechmann
Series Designer: Emily Love

Photo credits: Rex Features/AP Images, cover, 3; Mark Halmas/Icon SMI, 6; Mike Segar/Pool/AP Images, 9; Allen Eyestone/ABACAUSA.COM/Newscom, 12; Crosnier/DPPI-SIPA/ICON SMI, 14, 100; Seth Poppel/Yearbook Library, 18, 30, 96 (top); Zuma Press/Icon SMI, 20, 87, 88; Jorge Rios iPhoto Inc./Newscom, 22; Everett/REX USA, 25; LionsGate/Everett Collection, 29, 97; Lions Gate/Everett/REX USA, 36; Michael J. Le Brecht II/NewSport/Corbis, 39; Phil Masturzo KRT/Newscom, 40, 45, 52; Tony Dejak/AP Images, 48; Ron Kuntz/Reuters/Newscom, 58; Lucy Nicholson/Reuters/Newscom, 61; Icon Sports Media, 62, 96 (bottom); Detroit Free Press/ZUMA Press/Icon SMI, 68; Amy Sancetta/AP Images, 71, 99 (top); Andrew Weber/Icon SMI, 72, 98; Camera 4/Imago/Icon SMI, 75; Lori Shepler/AP Images, 79; Greenwich Time/Bob Luckey/AP Images, 80; J.Pat Carter/AP Images, 83; Lynne Sladky/AP Images, 92; MCT/ZUMA Press/Icon SMI, 95, 99 (bottom)

Library of Congress Control Number: 2013946051

Cataloging-in-Publication Data

Bodden, Valerie.
 LeBron James: champion basketball star / Valerie Bodden.
   p. cm. -- (Contemporary lives)
Includes bibliographical references and index.
ISBN 978-1-62403-224-0
1. James, LeBron--Juvenile literature. 2. Basketball players--United States--Biography--Juvenile literature. 3. African American basketball players-- Biography--Juvenile literature. 1. Title.
796.323092--dc23
[B]
                                                     2013946051

CONTENTS

In the moments before Game 5 of the 2012 NBA Finals, LeBron James readied himself with intense focus and determination.

CHAPTER 1

Champion at Last

||||||||||||||||||||||||||||||||||||||||||||

The crowd at AmericanAirlines Arena in Miami, Florida, roared as LeBron James and the Miami Heat took the court. It was Game 5 of the 2012 National Basketball Association (NBA) Finals. The Heat led the series 3–1 against the Oklahoma City Thunder. A win in Game 5 would clinch the championship for James and the Heat.

So far, the series had been hard fought. The Thunder's leader was Kevin Durant, whom many ranked as the second-best basketball player in the league, after James. Although the Thunder had a less experienced lineup, it was favored to win the series.

The Heat fell to the Thunder 105–94 in the first game. But the Heat rallied in Game 2, taking the lead from the start. In the final seconds of the game, James prevented Durant from tying the score. Then James made two free throws to cap the 100–96 win. At their next matchup in Game 3, the Thunder kept it close, but the Heat again came out ahead with a 91–85 victory.

In Game 4, the Thunder pulled to an early lead. But by late in the fourth quarter, the Heat led by two points and held on for the win. Miami's 104–98 victory in Game 4 meant James needed to win only one more game to clinch his first NBA championship.

||||||||||||||||||||||||||||||||||||||||||||||||||||||||||

James made an electrifying dunk to kick off Game 5.

KING OF THE COURT

Game 5 got off to a fast start. Within seconds of the tip-off, James dunked to score the game's first points. By halftime, he had scored 15 points, helping pull the Heat to a 59–49 lead. Although the Thunder briefly rallied in the third quarter to pull within seven points, James and the Heat answered. Heavily covered by the Thunder's defenders, James passed to open shooters, including fellow star players Dwyane Wade and Chris Bosh.

Focused throughout the entire game, James showed little emotion, not even pausing to celebrate after great plays. As the game clock wound down, James finally let his emotions show, hopping up and down and smiling. At the buzzer, the score was 121–106. The Miami Heat had won the 2012 NBA championship. Confetti showered the arena.

Even in this celebratory moment, James showed great sportsmanship when he rushed midcourt to hug Durant and offer him words of encouragement. "I told him he's unbelievable," James said. "I told him he shouldn't feel any regrets. And I told him to continue to work. I hope it's us and them every year."[1]

IIIIIIIIIIIIIIIIIIIIIIIIIIIIIIIIIIIIIIIIIIIIIIIIIIII

A LONG ROAD

"This right here is the happiest day of my life. This is a dream come true," James said after his team received the Larry O'Brien NBA Championship Trophy.[2] He had been waiting for this moment

Before taking the floor for Game 5 of the 2012 Finals, James gave his team a pep talk: "If someone came to you right now and told you, 'If you don't win tonight you won't see your family again,' how would you play? Approach this game like your family is in danger. How bad do you want to see your family again?"[3] His dire message spoke to the urgency of winning the game and clinching the title.

since he entered the NBA nine years earlier. He had been in the Finals twice before. Both times, he had come up short. He and the Heat had lost the 2011 Finals the year before, and he had also lost the 2007 Finals with the Cleveland Cavaliers. But now, he had earned his first NBA championship ring. He had also earned his first Bill Russell NBA Finals Most Valuable Player (MVP) Award. He had worked hard for it, scoring a triple-double in Game 5, with 26 points, 11 rebounds, and 13 assists.

The Heat's victory was extra sweet, coming on the heels of a difficult season the year before. It felt as if the entire country were rooting against James and the Heat. Many were angered by the way James had left his hometown Cavaliers to join

James could hardly believe his eyes as he looked upon the championship trophy in his hands.

a star-studded team with Wade and Bosh. Others were annoyed with James's declaration that Miami would win not one championship, "not two, not three, not four, not five, not six, not seven," but even more.[4] When the Heat lost the 2011 Finals, James's critics rejoiced.

After losing in 2011, James took a hard look at his game and his attitude. "It took me to go all the way to the top and then hit rock bottom to realize what I needed to do as a professional athlete and a person," he said.[5] He admitted, "I played [in 2011] to prove people wrong instead of just playing my game, instead of just going out and having fun and playing a game that I grew up loving."[6]

THE NEXT CHALLENGE

James's changed perspective paid off with the 2012 championship. The way he rededicated himself to the sport also regained him a measure of respect in many people's eyes. And his performance in the 2012 Finals proved he could stand up to the pressure of big moments and big games.

But even as he celebrated his championship, James was ready for the next challenge. "I know I can get better," he said. "And I know I'm not satisfied with one of these."[7]

AMONG THE BEST

James's MVP award for the Finals was well earned. During the span of the 2012 play-offs, James scored 25 points or more in all but two games. That made him only the third player ever to score 25 points in at least 20 games in a single postseason. The other two players were Michael Jordan and Hakeem Olajuwon. Altogether, James scored 697 points during the 2012 postseason, making him the postseason points leader that year.

Superstar LeBron James has come a long way from his childhood in poor, rough neighborhoods of Akron, Ohio.

CHAPTER 2

Tough Start

||||||||||||||||||||||||||||||||||||||||||||||||||||||||||||||||||||||||||||

LeBron Raymone James was born on December 30, 1984, in Akron, Ohio. His mother, Gloria James, was only 16 years old when LeBron was born. He never knew his father, Anthony McClelland. Eddie Jackson, his mother's sometimes-boyfriend, served as a father figure at times. But Jackson was not always around, as he spent time in and out of jail on fraud and drug charges.

While she raised LeBron, Gloria lived with her mother, Freda. Gloria's two brothers also lived with them. Their home was on Hickory Street in a rough neighborhood of Akron. Empty lots nearby served as dumping grounds for unwanted items such as tires and refrigerators. The older kids in the neighborhood used a milk crate hung from a telephone pole as a basketball hoop.

When LeBron was three, his grandmother died of a heart attack. It was Christmas morning. But

AKRON

In the 1920s, Akron, Ohio, was dubbed the "Rubber Capital of the World." Tire manufacturers such as Firestone, General Tire, Goodrich, and Goodyear had headquarters in Akron. The rubber factories provided employment to thousands. By the time LeBron was born in 1984, however, many of the factories had closed. Akron had fallen on hard times. Instead of a booming industrial center, Akron had become a forgotten city of 225,000 people.[1]

LeBron was always bothered by the fact that Akron wasn't even on most US maps. In his autobiography, *LeBron's Dream Team*, he said that as a kid, he resolved to do something about that: "I promised myself, in the funny way that little kids make promises over things that nobody else in the world cares about, that one day I was going to put Akron on the map.... I didn't know how. I just knew in my heart I was going to do it."[2]

Gloria did not tell LeBron the news until after he had opened his presents—which included his first toy basketball hoop. She wanted him to enjoy Christmas before hearing the devastating news.

Although Gloria and her brothers tried to manage the house after their mother's death, they could not afford to fix its many problems. Eventually, the city of Akron ordered the house be torn down, and Gloria and LeBron had to find a new place to live.

ON THE MOVE

Unable to get a place of their own, LeBron and Gloria moved from one friend's house to another. They never stayed in one place long. By the time he was eight, LeBron had moved 12 times.[3] Many of the friends Gloria and LeBron stayed with lived in the Elizabeth Park projects. The projects were a rough place, where the sounds of gunshots and police cars filled the nights.

In order to make ends meet, LeBron's mom took whatever jobs she could, often working nights. LeBron worried that one night she might

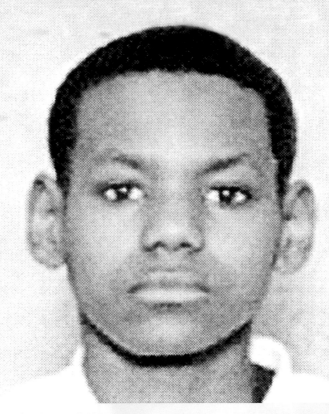

Young LeBron did his best to avoid the trouble and danger that often came from living in the projects.

not make it home. Alcohol and drugs were a constant presence in the projects as well. "It was scary but I never got into none of that stuff. That just wasn't me. . . . I knew it was wrong," he said.[4]

Moving from one place to another meant LeBron frequently switched schools. Although he easily made new friends, LeBron knew he'd soon be on the move again, leaving those friends behind. Sometimes Gloria had no way to get LeBron to school during these times. In fourth grade, he was absent almost 100 days.[5]

STARTING SPORTS

Soon after getting his first basketball hoop when he was three, LeBron learned how to dunk. By the time he was eight or nine, it was clear he had significant athletic talents. He began playing for a local football team called the East Dragons. In just six games, he scored 18 touchdowns. LeBron began to dream of someday playing in the National Football League (NFL).

IDOLS AND INSPIRATIONS

Growing up, LeBron did not root for his local sports teams. Instead, he rooted for the Chicago Bulls, the Dallas Cowboys, the Florida State Seminoles, and the New York Yankees. The teams were some of the most successful and talented of the 1980s and 1990s.

LeBron especially idolized Michael Jordan of the Bulls. Now retired, Jordan is still widely regarded as one of the best basketball players of all time. It wasn't long before people made comparisons between Jordan and LeBron. At first, LeBron encouraged those comparisons. In high school and his early years in the NBA, he chose to wear number 23, as Jordan had worn with the Bulls. He would later change his number in 2010.

As a struggling single mother, Gloria James, seen here in 2013, accepted Coach Walker's offer to help LeBron and provide him more stability.

Around the same time, LeBron began playing basketball on a recreation-league team called the Summit Lake Hornets. Although he preferred to play football, LeBron also had a natural talent for basketball. And he learned very quickly. Coach Frankie Walker of the Hornets was amazed with LeBron's ability.

A SENSE OF STABILITY

Noticing Gloria was struggling to provide a stable environment for LeBron, Coach Walker offered to look after him until she was more settled. Gloria agreed, and LeBron moved in with the Walker family. During his fifth-grade year in 1995, LeBron stayed with the Walkers during the week and with his mom on weekends.

LeBron soon began to feel he was part of the Walker family. The three Walker children treated him like a brother. Frankie and his wife, Pam, treated him like a son, including when it came to discipline. The Walkers expected him to go to school—every day. LeBron had perfect attendance in fifth grade. He discovered he even liked school and was a good student. "The Walkers laid a foundation for me, a foundation I really had never experienced before. I got the stability I craved," he stated.[6]

By the time LeBron was in sixth grade, his mother had found a home in Spring Hill Apartments, a housing complex in Akron. LeBron moved back in with her during the week and spent weekends with the Walkers. Although their apartment was tiny, LeBron and Gloria were grateful to finally have their own place. LeBron had his own room, which he decorated with posters of his basketball heroes, Michael Jordan and Kobe Bryant. He could only dream of where his life would take him someday.

||||||||||

To this day, James, *second from left*, remains close to the friends he first made as a Shooting Star.

CHAPTER 3

Shooting Star

||||||||||||||||||||||||||||||||||||||||||||||||||||||||||||||||||||||||||||||||||||||||||||

I n 1996, LeBron joined a new
basketball team known as the
Shooting Stars. The Shooting Stars
were part of the Amateur Athletic
Union (AAU), which organizes amateur
tournaments in several different sports.
Coach Dru Joyce II had seen LeBron play
for the Hornets, and he asked LeBron to
join the Shooting Stars. Joyce was excited
about LeBron's skill. LeBron was excited
about the possibility of traveling with the
team to places such as Cleveland. He had

never visited the larger city before, even though it was only 30 minutes away.

Other members of the team included Coach Joyce's son Dru Joyce III, known as Little Dru, and Sian Cotton, who was big and could play defense. Joyce taught the young boys more than basketball. He became a father figure and guide. LeBron said, "What Coach Dru did for us was set up life for us after the game of basketball in a way I cannot explain."[1]

NATIONAL CHAMPIONSHIP TOURNAMENTS

LeBron and his teammates played well their first year together. At the end of the season, the

SHOOT LESS, PASS MORE

One of the first things Joyce taught LeBron was that other players on the team could score points too. Learning to pass would make LeBron a well-rounded player. Joyce encouraged LeBron to shoot less and pass more. After just one discussion, LeBron understood and followed direction immediately. "That was the last time that I ever had to talk about LeBron shooting too much. He just got it. He started passing the ball," Joyce said.[2]

As a member of the Shooting Stars, LeBron, *second from right*, found the camaraderie he needed.

Shooting Stars qualified for the AAU national tournament in Cocoa Beach, Florida. The team crammed into Joyce's van for the 1,000-mile (1,600 km) drive. The Shooting Stars surprised everyone, finishing ninth out of 64 teams in the tournament.

After the summer tournament, LeBron entered sixth grade at Riedinger Middle School. He was a dedicated student. He always turned in his homework and often made the merit and honor rolls with a grade point average of 3.0 or higher.

In sixth grade, LeBron returned to the Shooting Stars. The team qualified for the 1997 AAU national tournament held in Salt Lake City, Utah. They managed to raise enough money to buy plane tickets for the trip. The Shooting Stars played hard and finished tenth.

||||||||||||||||||||||||||||||||||||||||||||||||||||

GROWING FRIENDSHIP

The next year, the Shooting Stars added a new member, Willie McGee. Willie quickly became friends with LeBron, Little Dru, and Sian. The boys spent as much time together off the court as on it. They shared pizza and candy, played video games at Little Dru's house, or shot hoops in his driveway.

That year, the Shooting Stars played approximately 60 games, many of them out of state in West Virginia and Indiana. When they were on the road, the boys often stayed up into the early morning hours, even before games.

For the national tournament, the Shooting Stars traveled to Memphis, Tennessee. But when they got there, LeBron and his teammates got distracted and didn't stay focused off court. They instead spent too much time by the pool and with other kids. They were eliminated from the tournament in an early game.

The Shooting Stars used that loss as motivation for the 1999 season. This time, the national tournament was in Orlando, Florida, the home of Walt Disney World and other theme parks. Even with those potential distractions, LeBron and his teammates remained focused. They stayed away from theme parks and even the hotel pool.

The renewed focus paid off. The Shooting Stars made it all the way to the final game of the national tournament. There they met the Southern California All-Stars, a team that had won the national championship the previous three years. The game was close. With 12 seconds remaining, the All-Stars held only a two-point lead. LeBron got the ball and took a three-point shot at the buzzer. It rolled around the rim and looked as if it would go in. But at the last second, the ball rolled back out, and the Shooting Stars lost.

GETTING READY FOR HIGH SCHOOL

LeBron and his friends graduated from eighth grade in 1999. Most people assumed they would go to Buchtel High School, which had a reputation for strong athletics and a primarily black student body. But the Buchtel coaches made it clear they would not place Little Dru on the varsity team if the friends chose that school.

Instead, Little Dru decided to attend Saint Vincent-Saint Mary, a small Catholic school with a primarily white student body. The Shooting Stars knew Coach Keith Dambrot through basketball clinics held at Akron's Jewish community center.

COACH DAMBROT

Before holding basketball clinics at the Jewish community center in Akron, Keith Dambrot served as head coach at Central Michigan University. But he was fired in 1993 after using a racial slur. When LeBron and his friends considered playing for Dambrot at Saint Vincent-Saint Mary, Dambrot met with their parents to discuss his firing. He explained he had asked his Central Michigan University players' permission to use the term and had not used it in a negative sense. Neither LeBron nor his friends ever had a problem with discrimination or racial prejudice from Dambrot.

Despite some criticism, LeBron, *second from left*, chose to attend Saint Vincent-Saint Mary High School with his friends.

After talking about it for several weeks, the four friends decided Saint Vincent-Saint Mary was the school for all of them. Their decision was not a popular one among Akron's black community, which saw the boys as traitors for not attending Buchtel. But the community's anger only fired the boys' desire to win. LeBron was now ready for what high school would bring both on and off the court.

||||||||||||

As a freshman, LeBron adjusted to a new school while he brought his game to a new level.

CHAPTER 4

High School Days

||||||||||||||||||||||||||

LeBron was in for a surprise when he walked through the doors of St. Vincent-St. Mary for his first day of school in fall 1999. "I came through that door, and thought, 'Wow, there might be a problem,'" he later said.[1] More than 85 percent of Saint Vincent-Saint Mary's students were white, but LeBron had rarely spent time with white people.[2] He explained:

I didn't know anything at all about their culture. I didn't know whether it was the same as ours or different, or what. I didn't think I made a mistake, but it was a big transition.[3]

Although LeBron was at first uncomfortable, he soon adjusted to the new environment, and most Saint Vincent-Saint Mary students accepted him and his friends.

The rules at the Catholic school were different from the rules at LeBron's previous schools. For the first time in his life, he had to follow a dress code. That meant dress pants, a belt, a shirt with a collar, and dress shoes. Soon after starting high school, LeBron got his first tattoo—a lion on his right

INK

LeBron got his first tattoo at the age of 15 because he wanted to be like Allen Iverson, the highly inked basketball star who played for the Philadelphia 76ers. It would be the first of many tattoos for LeBron. After a *Sports Illustrated* article dubbed LeBron the "Chosen One" in 2002, he had "Chosen 1" tattooed across his back.[4] He later had his first son's face and second son's name tattooed on his arm. Other arm tattoos include his mother's name; an image of a beast; and Akron's area code, "330." He also has "Family" on his abdomen and "Witness" and "History" on his calves.[5]

arm. But during school hours, he had to wear long sleeves to cover it up. The tattoo also had to be covered with a white patch for basketball games.

Saint Vincent-Saint Mary was known for its strong academics, and LeBron was expected to keep his grades up. Even with these high expectations, he did not struggle in his new school. As he had since fifth grade, he always made sure to turn his homework in on time. He maintained a grade point average of approximately 2.8.

ON THE FIELD AND ON THE COURT

At six feet four inches (1.93 m) and 170 pounds (77.11 kg), LeBron had the perfect build for a football player. He joined Saint Vincent-Saint Mary's football team, along with Sian and Willie Although he started out on the freshman team, LeBron was soon promoted to junior varsity and then to varsity. He was active in the play-offs, catching eight passes in a single game.

After the football season, it was time for LeBron and his friends to do what they had come to

Saint Vincent-Saint Mary to do. They took to the basketball court under the direction of Dambrot. LeBron was surprised the patient coach he had known at the Jewish community center had transformed into a "madman. . . . He screamed. He demanded. He cussed."[6] At first, LeBron and his friends thought they had made a mistake in coming to Saint Vincent-Saint Mary to play for Dambrot, but they soon realized he was good for their game.

A reporter nicknamed LeBron, Little Dru, Sian, and Willie the "Fab Four." The Fab Four were joined on the court by Maverick Carter, a

OTHER "FAB" GROUPS ||||||||||||||||||||||||||||||||||||||||||||||||||||||||||||

LeBron and his friends were nicknamed the "Fab Four," but they were not the first to carry the "Fab" name. In 1991, the University of Michigan basketball team recruited a group of players who came to be known as the "Fab Five." The group reached the National Collegiate Athletic Association (NCAA) championship game in both their freshman and sophomore seasons. With baggy shorts and hip-hop style, they were controversial. Some hailed them as the new, young generation of basketball players. Others felt they were thuggish. But years before them, the "Fab Four" originated as a nickname for the Beatles, the legendary rock group of the 1960s.

senior who had been friends with LeBron since childhood. Although Maverick was the team's leader, LeBron started even as a freshman. In his first high school game, LeBron scored 15 points as the Saint Vincent-Saint Mary Fighting Irish defeated Cuyahoga Falls 76–40.

LeBron's season average was 18 points per game, but his coaches felt it could be even higher. According to Steve Culp, one of the Fighting Irish's assistant coaches, if there was one problem with LeBron, it was convincing him to shoot more. He said, "People would tell him that he should score more points, or he should do this or that. LeBron was confident enough in himself and his game to ignore that."[7]

LeBron's basketball smarts and team-first attitude led the Fighting Irish to an undefeated 20–0 regular-season record his freshman year. In March 2000, the team played in the state championship before a crowd of thousands at Ohio State University. They defeated Greeneview High School 73–55 to take home Saint Vincent-Saint Mary's first state championship in 16 years.

With LeBron's talent and leadership, the Fighting Irish took the 2000 state championship.

SOPHOMORE STARS

The summer after his freshman year, LeBron played in a number of basketball tournaments around the country. In the fall, he was again on the football field. He had an amazing season, making 42 receptions for 820 yards and seven touchdowns. By the end of the season, major colleges were calling to recruit LeBron to play football after graduation.

But LeBron was beginning to see his future was in basketball. At the start of the basketball season, the Fab Four were joined by a new teammate, Romeo Travis. Although LeBron had gone to the same middle school as Romeo, the rest of the Fab Four did not get along with their new team member. They believed he was selfish both on and off the court.

Despite the friction, the Fighting Irish again excelled during LeBron's sophomore year. By now, they were determined to win not just a state championship but a national championship. In high school basketball, the national championship is determined by *USA Today* rankings rather than a national play-off. The only way for them to win a national championship was to beat the country's

A MOTHER'S SUPPORT

LeBron's mom, Gloria, loved to root for her son. At games, she wore a Saint Vincent-Saint Mary jersey with "LeBron's Mom" printed across the back. Often, she mocked fans of the opposing team. In return, opposing fans sometimes booed her antics. LeBron never worried about his mom's antics at the games. He knew it was just a sign of her love and support. "Whatever my mom could do or could not do, I also knew that nobody was more important in her life than I was," he said.[8]

top-ranked teams, so the Fighting Irish took on a tough schedule that included powerhouse teams from Virginia, Wisconsin, and Michigan.

Ten games into the season, the Fighting Irish met Oak Hill Academy from Virginia, one of the best high school basketball teams in the country. A win against Oak Hill would put Saint Vincent-Saint Mary at number one in the *USA Today* rankings. Although LeBron and his teammates took an early lead, they couldn't hold on in the final minutes. With only seconds left and Oak Hill leading by one, LeBron took a shot. The ball spun around the rim, but then it popped back out. LeBron was devastated. Although he had scored 33 points and was named MVP of the game, his only goal had been to win.

|||||||||||||||||||||||||||||||||||||||||||||||||||||

GETTING NOTICED

Despite the loss against Oak Hill, LeBron was beginning to attain star status. A Chicago Bulls scout was at the game to check out Oak Hill star DeSagana Diop. The scout couldn't help but notice LeBron. Soon there were rumors that LeBron might

Each year, LeBron further separated himself from other players his age.

go right to the NBA after high school, rather than playing for a college team first.

Local newspaper reporters called LeBron "King James," and huge crowds turned out to watch him play. After finishing the 2000–01 season with only one loss, LeBron and the Fighting Irish played in the state championship game before a record crowd. They won the title for the second year in a row. They finished fifth in the *USA Today* poll. At the end of the season, LeBron was named Mr. Basketball of Ohio, an award for the best high school player in the state. Although LeBron took it all in stride, he didn't know how much more attention he would soon get.

IIIIIIIII

As high school continued, LeBron gained more and more attention for his dominance on the court.

CHAPTER 5

National Attention

|||||||||||||||||||||||||||||||||||||||||||||||||||||||||

LeBron spent the summer of 2001 playing at basketball camps and tournaments around the country. But when fall came around, he once again put on his football pads. LeBron knew getting hurt on the football field could end his NBA career before it started. But he also knew he loved football and high school was a time for having fun.

During the summer of 2001, LeBron was invited to a workout Michael Jordan was hosting in Chicago. He was in awe: "When he walked in, it was like, I didn't know what to say. It was overwhelming to meet—you know, to finally meet—the guy I've looked up to my whole life."[1] Although LeBron didn't get to talk to his idol much that day, he did get to practice with other NBA stars. The following February, Jordan attended one of LeBron's games in Akron, and the two had an opportunity to chat. Jordan gave the high schooler some pointers: "One dribble, stop and pull up. That's what I want to see. . . . That's my guy."[2]

LeBron's football coaches were careful to keep him from getting hurt. He was never hit in practice, and when he made a reception, he ran out of bounds to avoid getting tackled. LeBron ended his junior season with 61 receptions for 1,245 yards and 16 touchdowns.

||||||||||||||||||||||||||||||||||||||||||||||||||||||

CHANGES

After football season, LeBron returned to the basketball court. But there had been some changes since his sophomore season. Dambrot had left Saint Vincent-Saint Mary to take a position as an assistant coach at the University of Akron. Dru Joyce II, the boys' former Shooting Stars coach, had been serving as an assistant coach at Saint Vincent-Saint Mary for two years. Now he would take over as head coach.

In many ways, Joyce was the opposite of Dambrot. Whereas Dambrot had yelled at the players, Joyce gently encouraged them. LeBron and the others—including Little Dru, Joyce's own son—did not take well to the new style. They began treating Joyce disrespectfully, sometimes even refusing to follow his orders.

Despite their poor attitude toward their coach, the Fighting Irish continued to win. They weren't winning as easily, though. Joyce warned they weren't playing up to their potential. They refused to listen.

|||||||||||||||||||||||||||||||||||||||||||||||||||||||||||||||||

"THE CHOSEN ONE"

The Fighting Irish had become so popular home games were now being played at the James A. Rhodes Arena at the University of Akron, which seated more people. LeBron mania only increased with the February 18, 2002, issue of *Sports Illustrated*, which featured LeBron on the cover. The headline was, "The Chosen One."[3] The article touted him as the best player since Jordan, calling him "Air Apparent" to "Air Jordan."[4]

Suddenly, everyone wanted LeBron's autograph. Reporters began attending Saint Vincent-Saint Mary games. They tried to approach LeBron at practices. So did people from companies hoping to sponsor LeBron once he went pro. Joyce finally had to close practices to outsiders. The school was also closed to media during school hours.

||||||||||||||||||||||||||||||||||||||||||||||||||||||||||||||

"They . . . had no stars in their eyes about me like so many others did. Their attitude was, 'You're still LeBron James. Don't put on any airs with us, we know who you are.' They never glorified me."[5]

—LEBRON JAMES ON HOW HE RELIED ON HIS FRIENDS TO KEEP HIM GROUNDED

HEARTBREAKING LOSS

The widespread attention—along with drivers' licenses—distracted LeBron and his teammates

Only a junior, LeBron was bombarded by national media attention, awards, and speculation.

from their mission of winning a national championship. They rarely stayed at practice any longer than they had to, and they continued giving Joyce a hard time. The boys began partying until 4:00 or 5:00 a.m., even before game days. They behaved the same way the night before the state finals—and paid the price, losing 71–63. For the first time in LeBron's high school basketball career, the Fighting Irish were not the state champions. They were not even ranked in the top 25 in *USA Today*'s national poll.

A NEW FOCUS

In the summer of 2002, LeBron broke his wrist during a basketball tournament. The injury made him realize how quickly his basketball career could come to an end. He decided not to risk playing football in the fall. He still attended football games to cheer on his team, however. At one game, he met 16-year-old Savannah Brinson. Although Savannah attended a different school, LeBron asked her out, and the two soon began dating.

LeBron now knew he would go right into the NBA after high school instead of going to college. It was a decision few high schoolers could even consider—few were as talented and NBA-ready as LeBron.

LeBron still focused on his schoolwork, despite knowing he didn't need good grades for college admissions. He said, "I have too much pride to go into a class where everybody else is doing their work and not have my work done."[6] His hard work earned him a GPA above 3.0 his senior year.

LeBron knew this was his last year to earn a national championship with the Fighting Irish. The Fab Four decided their team needed to get

The vast majority of basketball prospects need to mature and develop in college before they are ready for the NBA. But with his extraordinary talent and skill, LeBron was ready to enter the NBA immediately after high school.

In decades past, only a handful of individuals, such as Moses Malone, played professional basketball without first attending college. It was a rare practice. Then in 1995, Kevin Garnett entered the NBA draft immediately after high school, and Kobe Bryant did the same in 1996. Both were first-round draft picks. They sparked a number of other players to follow the path straight to the NBA, although to varying degrees of success. LeBron is considered perhaps the most successful of the group. As Gerald Green, a 2013 high school draftee noted, "There's only one LeBron James. He came in ready and he dominated the league."[7]

Green carries a special distinction as well. He will likely be the last 18-year-old drafted into the NBA. The NBA now requires draftees to be at least 19 years old and one year removed from high school.

along better. They officially invited Romeo to join their group, making them the Fab Five. The team traveled to California, New Jersey, North Carolina, and Pennsylvania to play top teams in the country. A couple games were even broadcast live on the cable sports network ESPN2.

On LeBron's eighteenth
birthday, the gift of a Hummer
H2 sparked an investigation.

BIRTHDAY AND SCANDAL

LeBron turned 18 on December 30, 2002. He celebrated with a party—and a brand-new Hummer H2 SUV from his mom. Although LeBron was thrilled with his new ride, the gift immediately raised a red flag with the Ohio High School Athletic Association. Members of the association knew Gloria had little money and the vehicle had cost more than $50,000.[8] They wondered if the Hummer was a gift from an agent or a sponsor. Accepting such a gift would have made LeBron ineligible to play amateur basketball in high school. A two-week investigation revealed Gloria's Hummer purchase was legitimate. Gloria herself had secured a loan for the vehicle against her son's future earnings.

Only days after the Hummer controversy cleared, LeBron faced another scandal. This time, the state athletic association had learned LeBron had accepted two jerseys worth $845 from a local store.[9] After only one day of investigation, the athletic association declared LeBron ineligible for the rest of his senior season.

LeBron's mother fought the ruling with the help of lawyer Fred Nance. They argued the jerseys had been given as a reward for academic rather than athletic performance. He also said the athletic association had failed to make a thorough investigation before declaring LeBron ineligible. A judge agreed and ruled LeBron was eligible to finish his senior season. However, he ordered LeBron be suspended two games. The Fighting Irish won both of those games without their star. And in his first game after the suspension, LeBron scored a career-high 52 points.

|||||||||||||||||||||||||||||||||||||||||||||||||||||||||||||

SENIOR NIGHT ||||||||||||||||||||||||||||||||||||||||||||||||||||||||||||||||||||||||||||||||||||||

Nearly all of Saint Vincent-Saint Mary's home games were played at the University of Akron during LeBron's senior year. But LeBron and his teammates requested they be allowed to play at their own school gym for senior night. It was a night when all the seniors on the team would be introduced and honored, along with their families.

When it came time for LeBron to be recognized, his mom was not there. She was handling the police report and paperwork for an accident LeBron had gotten into with his Hummer earlier that day. Because Gloria couldn't be there, LeBron's teammates—whom he considered brothers—left their own parents' sides to escort their friend onto the court.

NATIONAL CHAMPIONS

Despite the scandals, LeBron and his teammates remained focused on the court and continued to win. In the state finals on March 22, they faced Archbishop Alter High School. With a score of 40–36, the Fab Five won their last game together. The Fighting Irish were state champions for the third time in four years. The win also gave them the number one spot on the *USA Today* poll. They had finally achieved their dream of becoming national champions.

The next month, on April 26, LeBron officially announced he would enter the 2003 NBA draft. Throughout the spring, LeBron spent much of his time meeting with representatives from Reebok, Adidas, and Nike, all of whom wanted him to sign an endorsement deal. LeBron ultimately decided to sign with Nike, which offered him approximately $90 million for a seven-year contract.[10]

On June 7, 2003, LeBron graduated from Saint Vincent-Saint Mary. The next day, he left Akron to attend an NBA predraft camp in Chicago. He was ready for the big time.

|||||||||||

In a dream come true, James was selected first overall in the 2003 NBA draft.

CHAPTER 6

NBA Bound

||||||||||||||||||||||||||||||||||||||||||||||||||||||||||||||||||||||||||||||||||||||

The Cleveland Cavaliers had the first pick in the 2003 NBA draft, which was held on June 26. It was no surprise when they used that pick to bring LeBron James to their franchise. Being the first-overall pick spoke volumes about James's talent at such a young age—as well as the potential he could achieve as he grew older.

James had never been a Cavaliers fan. Nonetheless, the Akron native was

In May 2003, the Cavaliers learned they would have the top pick for the 2003 draft. Many fans, realizing that pick would be James, immediately called to order season tickets. Thousands of Cavs fans filled the stands at Gund Arena to watch an ESPN broadcast of the draft on June 26. When the Cavs selected James, confetti rained down on cheering fans, almost as if the team had just won a championship.

James's arrival brought new hope to a city that had not won a championship in any professional sport since 1964. With James on the team, crowds of more than 18,000 filled the stands, up from 11,000 before James arrived.[2] An intimidating billboard of James met opposing teams outside the arena. Local businesses also benefited from the increased traffic into the city.

thrilled to be playing for his hometown team. His three-year contract with the Cavs was worth approximately $13 million.[1]

James soon hit the gym to practice with his coach, Paul Silas, who was also new to the Cavaliers for the 2003–04 season. Silas was pleasantly surprised to find James had not developed a bad attitude as a result of his celebrity status. "LeBron was wise beyond his years. . . . He was willing to learn. In terms of attitude, you could not have asked for more," Silas said.[3]

TROUBLED TEAM

Before picking James, the Cavaliers had had a horrible 2002–03 season, with a record of 65 losses and only 17 wins. They had been a losing team for so many years, few good players were willing to join or stay with the franchise. Only one of James's teammates—center Zydrunas Ilgauskas—was all-star caliber.

For James, whose high school teammates had been like brothers, playing for the Cavaliers was a lonely experience at first. Some of his teammates seemed to purposely ignore him. Even so, James quickly became a leader on the team. At practices, he was the first to understand the plays Silas wanted to run. He patiently ran those plays over and over until the rest of the team understood them too.

Before joining the NBA, James had always played the position of small forward, which generally focuses on scoring. But the Cavaliers had no point guard—a position that usually focuses on passing so teammates can score. So James volunteered to play the position. Although he played point guard for only half the season, James's offer won his teammates' respect. They began to treat him as part of the Cavaliers family.

||||||||||||||||||||||||||||||||||||||||||||||||||||||||

ROOKIE OF THE YEAR

James's first regular-season game was on October 29, 2003, against the Sacramento Kings. Although the Cavaliers lost the matchup 106–92, James earned 25 points, nine assists, and six rebounds. The Cavs played their first home game of the season on November 5 against the Denver Nuggets. Celebrities such as baseball star Ken Griffey Jr. and rapper Jay Z were in attendance.

"This is the biggest regular-season game we've ever had here. There was a buzz around the city. . . . This is great for the league. We all need him. He's a breath of fresh air."[4]

—SACRAMENTO KINGS OWNER JOE MALOOF ON JAMES PLAYING IN SACRAMENTO FOR HIS NBA DEBUT

Again, the Cavaliers lost. It was not until the sixth game of the season when the Cavaliers finally won, beating the Washington Wizards 111–98.

James sprained his ankle in January 2004 and had to sit out three games. When he got back onto the court, James started breaking records. On February 9, he became the youngest NBA player to reach 1,000 points. Then on March 27, he became the youngest player to score more than 40 points in a game.

By the end of the season, James had led the Cavaliers to a 35–47 record. It wasn't a winning record, but it was the best for the franchise in six years. James was named NBA Rookie of the Year on April 20. He was the youngest player to ever earn the award.

|||||||||||||||||||||||||||||||||||||||||||||||||||||||||||

BUSY OFF-SEASON

During the summer of 2004, James traveled to Athens, Greece, to play on the US men's basketball team in the Olympic Games. Although James was excited to represent his country, he was disappointed with the amount of playing time

After a spectacular first season with the Cavs, James was named Rookie of the Year.

he received. He and other young team members largely sat on the bench as more-experienced players took the court. James played approximately 12 minutes per game and averaged just over five points. Team USA, which had been expected to dominate the competition, took home the bronze medal. It was viewed as a major disappointment.

That fall, James experienced another milestone—this time, off the court. On October 6, 2004, James and his high school sweetheart, Savannah Brinson, welcomed a son, LeBron Jr. James said having a son changed his perspective on basketball:

> Sometimes in the past when I played something might make me lose focus, or I would go home after a game where I thought I could have played better and I would let it hang over my head.... But now, being a parent, I go home and see my son and I forget about any mistake I ever made or the reason I'm upset.[5]

"Now that I have a son, I have no idea how she did it by herself because I couldn't do it by myself."[6]

—JAMES, REFLECTING ON HIS MOTHER

Also off the court, James wanted to help others in his local community. In 2004, he formed the LeBron James Family Foundation. The foundation's mission was "to positively affect the lives of children and young adults" through programs promoting education and a healthy lifestyle.[7]

A NEW SEASON

Although the Cavs started the 2004–05 season with a three-game losing streak, they followed that with a six-game winning streak. Win or lose, James was hounded by the media.

The day before James's twentieth birthday, Dikembe Mutombo of the Houston Rockets accidentally elbowed him in the face. James suffered a broken cheekbone. He had to wear a clear face mask until the cheekbone healed, but James didn't let it affect his play. On January 19, 2005, he became the youngest player to ever post a triple-double. And on February 20, he played in his first All-Star Game, during which he passed off to veteran players rather than take shots himself. He explained, "My time in these games will come."[8]

In the middle of the season, the Cavaliers changed ownership. In March, new owner Dan Gilbert fired coach Paul Silas with 18 games left in

While he mostly just passed the ball during the 2005 All-Star Game, James also managed to make a few thrilling shots.

the season. Assistant coach Brendan Malone took over for the rest of the season.

Although the Cavs ended the season with a winning record of 42–40, they did not make the play-offs. This failure only increased James's determination.

||||||||||

James became captain of the Cavaliers in 2005, making him a leader on and off the court.

CHAPTER 7

Falling Short

IIIIIIIIIIIIIIIIIIIIIIIIIIIIIIIIIIIIIIIIIIIIIIIIIIIIIIIIIIIIIIIIIIIIIIIIIIIII

During the summer of 2005, the Cavaliers hired Mike Brown, a former assistant coach with the Indiana Pacers, as their new head coach. Brown immediately recruited talented shooters so James would no longer have to carry the team. He also made 20-year-old James the team captain. Although James was younger than his teammates, Brown felt he had the qualities needed to lead the team. The changes seemed to help. Although

Beginning in 2006, James starred in a Nike commercial series called *The LeBrons*. James helped develop the ad campaign, in which he played four different characters: Athlete LeBron, Wise LeBron, Business LeBron, and Kid LeBron. Each of the characters represented a different side of James's personality.

In the first ad of the campaign, the four LeBrons sit around the table eating dinner. The white-haired Wise LeBron brags to the others about his basketball achievements, claiming he once got a quadruple-double in a game. Business LeBron accuses him of lying, while Athlete LeBron shakes his head. Kid LeBron joyfully listens to music and digs into his meal.

The LeBrons was the first ad campaign in which James had a large speaking role. Afterward, other advertisers, including Coca-Cola and State Farm Insurance, used him in their own funny commercials.

the Cavs lost two of their first three games for the 2005–06 season, they then posted an eight-game winning streak.

Throughout the season, James was hotter than ever. He averaged a career-high 31.4 points per game. On January 21, 2006, James scored 51 points against the Utah Jazz and became the youngest player in the NBA to score 5,000 career points. On February 19, James played in his second All-Star Game. With 29 points, six rebounds, and two assists, he was named MVP of the game.

The Cavaliers finished the season with a 50–32 record—good enough to earn them a spot in the play-offs. James played in his first-ever NBA play-off game on April 22, 2006, against the Washington Wizards. He earned a triple-double—with 32 points, 11 rebounds, and 11 assists—as he led the Cavs to a 97–86 victory. They went on to win the series in six games. But they lost the Eastern Conference semifinals to the Detroit Pistons. Once again, their hopes for a championship were dashed.

||||||||||||||||||||||||||||||||||||||||||||||||||||||||

A LITTLE HELP FROM HIS FRIENDS

As James settled into his NBA career, he remained close to his high school friends. James's friends and business partners were often courtside for his games and helped him make career decisions. In the summer of 2006, when it came time for James to renegotiate his contract with the Cavaliers, he turned to his friends—including a new friend, rapper Jay Z—for advice.

James knew Cavaliers owner Gilbert had been working hard to keep him on the team. Gilbert had hired a team chef and outfitted players' lockers with televisions, stereos, and Xbox 360s. He had recruited players who would help James on the court. Even so, the Cavaliers had not yet won a championship, and that was what James wanted most.

James decided to sign a contract extension that guaranteed he would play with the Cavaliers for three more years. After that, he would reevaluate where he wanted to be.

||||||||||||||||||||||||||||||||||||||||||||||||||||||||||

A SHOT AT THE CHAMPIONSHIP

Before the 2006–07 season got underway, James wanted his teammates to know he was serious about winning a championship. At the first practice, James changed the team chant to "Championship."[1]

But as the season began, James's scoring seemed to suffer, especially in the final quarter of games. By the halfway point of the season, the Cavaliers had lost nearly as many games as they had won, with a 20–19 record. James said that instead of focusing on defense, he needed more freedom to score. Defense was important, James said, "but at the end of the day, if you don't put points on the board, you're not going to win basketball games."[2] In response, Brown gave James more offensive freedom, and the Cavs began to win more. They finished the season with a 50–32 record. Once again, they had earned a trip to the play-offs.

The Cavs swept the Wizards in the first round. They next defeated the New Jersey Nets in the Eastern Conference semifinals. They then won the Eastern Conference finals against the Pistons in six

EASTERN CONFERENCE FINALS |||||||||||||||||||||||||||||||

ESPN rated James's performance in Game 5 of the 2007 Eastern Conference finals as the fourth-best play-off performance of all time. Against the Pistons, James scored 48 points in the game, including 29 of the Cavaliers' last 30 points. The game went into double overtime, and James's scoring led to a 109–107 Cavs victory.

James became an offensive force in the 2007 play-offs, earning his first trip to the finals.

games. For the first time in his NBA career, James was on his way to the NBA Finals.

In the finals, James and the Cavs faced the San Antonio Spurs. The Spurs' tough defense kept

James from driving to the basket and forced him to make longer jump shots—many of which he missed. Although the Cavaliers put up a fight, the Spurs swept the series. James was crushed. "I have to be ten times better," he said afterward. "Our team has to be ten times better. . . . I have to be much better on and off the court, and that will carry our team to higher levels."[3]

A NEW ARRIVAL

Despite the disappointment of the loss, James had a reason to rejoice. Just after midnight on June 14—the night before Game 4 of the finals—Brinson gave birth to the couple's second son, Bryce Maximus.

"Once you become a professional athlete or once you do anything well, then you're automatically a role model. . . . I have no problem being a role model. I love it. I have kids looking up to me and hopefully I inspire these kids to do good things."[4]

—LEBRON JAMES ON BEING A ROLE MODEL TO HIS CHILDREN AND OTHERS

Although his basketball career often kept him on the road, James was an involved father. "He's just a great dad," Brinson said. James had a special bond with his boys. "If he was a child, they would be best friends."[5] For James, his sons helped him keep a sense of perspective and normalcy. "My sons . . . don't know if I missed the last three shots of the game or couldn't win the game or I turned the ball over," he said.[6] James's experiences in both life and basketball would only make him stronger for what lay ahead.

|||||||||

James could always turn to his family for support and perspective.

Off-season practice gave James
a leg up on what would turn
out to be an MVP season.

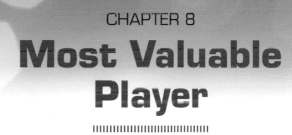

CHAPTER 8

Most Valuable Player

||||||||||||||||||||||||||||||||||||

After the Cavaliers' disappointing performance in the 2007 finals, James was serious when he said he needed to get better. Over the summer of 2007, he set out to do just that. Realizing his shooting had been inconsistent, he worked on his jump shot with Cavaliers assistant coach Chris Jent. Even when James went on vacation or needed to film a commercial, he brought Jent along to practice shooting. In addition, James lifted weights and practiced yoga.

Although he sat out five games in late November and early December due to a sprained finger, James's shooting remained impressive throughout the season. On February 27, 2008, James became the youngest player ever to score 10,000 career points. He made 48 percent of his shots from the field and averaged 30 points a game during the season. It earned him the NBA scoring title.

The Cavaliers finished the season 45–37 and again earned a spot in the play-offs. They made it through the first round, beating the Wizards in six games. They then faced the Boston Celtics in the Eastern Conference semifinals. They took the series to the last game, but they failed to pull out a win in Game 7. Yet again, there would be no NBA championship.

||||||||||||||||||||||||||||||||||||||||||||||||||||||||

BRINGING HOME THE GOLD

After another disappointing season with the Cavaliers, James returned to the US men's team

Winning a gold medal at the 2008 Olympics instilled James with pride.

for the 2008 Olympic Games in Beijing, China. James was now seen as a team leader. He embraced the role, saying, "It doesn't matter how good individuals are, if you don't have a leader, it's not going to be right. I took the responsibility from Day 1."[1]

Under James's leadership, the US team took home the gold medal and fulfilled their high expectations. James said it was one of the proudest moments of his life.

CHAMPIONSHIP OR FAILURE

As he approached the 2008–09 season, James was determined to finally win that elusive NBA championship. "I'm at a point in my career now, if I don't win an NBA championship, it's a failure," he said.[2] As part of his dedication to the game, James ensured he was in top physical condition. He was almost always the first one at practice and the last to leave.

James's dedication showed on the court. He scored 50 points or more in three games and averaged 28.4 points per game for the regular season. After leading the Cavs to a 66–16 record,

MORE THAN A GAME

While James's pro career was skyrocketing, memories from an earlier era came back to the forefront. Kristopher Belman, a film student from Akron, had filmed James and his teammates during their senior year of high school. Belman eventually developed the footage into *More Than a Game*, a full-length feature film. It debuted at the Toronto International Film Festival in September 2008. James said, "The point of the movie is about kids having a dream, setting a goal and sticking together, no matter what, to achieve that dream."[3]

the NBA's best record for the season, James was named league MVP on May 5, 2009.

James chose to hold the award ceremony at Saint Vincent-Saint Mary. The 24-year-old choked up as he thanked everyone who had helped him along the road to the MVP award: "Dreams do come true. . . . This is the place where all my dreams started, where I thought they could become real. There really isn't a better place."[4]

As James accepted his MVP award, the Cavaliers were in the middle of the play-offs. They swept the Pistons in the first round and the Atlanta Hawks in the Eastern Conference semifinals. But in the conference finals, the Orlando Magic pushed the Cavs out of the play-offs in six games.

James was disgusted with the 103–90 loss in Game 6. He walked off the court without shaking hands with the opposing team, an act many considered poor sportsmanship. James tried to explain his actions: "It's hard for me to congratulate somebody after you just lose to them."[5]

TEAMING UP WITH SHAQ

Nearing the end of his three-year extension, James would be a free agent after the 2009–10 season. So as the season approached, Cavaliers management was desperate to create a winning team and entice him to stay. In June 2009, they acquired Shaquille O'Neal from the Phoenix Suns. Considered one of the greatest players of his generation, O'Neal had already won four NBA championships. Although O'Neal was 37 years old, the Cavs hoped he could still help James win one.

Although the Cavs opened the season with back-to-back losses, by January 2010 they were in the middle of a 13-game winning streak. To add to game-day intensity, James created a ritual to bring the team together. Before each game, he sprinkled chalk powder on his hands and threw his arms up, letting the chalk fill the air above his head while the whole arena cheered wildly. James said it promoted "team chemistry and team camaraderie. . . . It's basically how we prepare for battle before we go out."[6]

The Cavs finished the season with a 61–21 record, once again the best in the NBA. Only a

In a thrilling ritual, James threw chalk powder into the air to signal his team's readiness.

year after winning his first MVP award, James took home another on May 2, 2010.

After winning the first round of the play-offs against the Bulls, the Cavaliers faced the Celtics in the Eastern Conference semifinals. James did not seem to be at the top of his game. The Cavs fell to the Celtics in six games. After Game 6, everyone in Cleveland wondered if James had played his last game as a Cavalier.

||||||||||

James announced the next step in his career during *The Decision*, a live ESPN special.

CHAPTER 9

The Decision

||||||||||||||||||||||||||||||||||||||||||||||||||||||||||||||||||||||

O n July 1, 2010, James became an unrestricted free agent. That meant he could stay with the Cavaliers or choose any team that offered him a contract. The entire basketball world speculated about his future. They wondered if he would remain with his hometown team or jump to a new team in a bigger market. As James remained tight-lipped about his options, rumors flew about him going to the Bulls, the Knicks, or the Heat. The Cavaliers held out hope he wasn't going anywhere.

On July 8, James held a live ESPN special called *The Decision* to announce where he would play. Even the Cavaliers' management would have to watch the special in order to learn what their star player had in mind. As fans in Cleveland—and everywhere—waited with bated breath, James announced, "This fall, I'm going to take my talents to South Beach and join the Miami Heat."[1]

BACKLASH

The Decision as a media event turned out to be a defining moment for James—a negative one. Many critics and sports fans blasted the special as "disastrous."[2] Although James gave more than $2.5 million in proceeds from the special to the Boys and Girls Clubs of America, the charitable act wasn't enough to win people over.[3]

The reaction in Cleveland was especially harsh. Fans burned James jerseys and threw rocks at the billboard of James in downtown Cleveland. Fans weren't the only ones upset. Cavaliers owner

As thousands of fans cheered, James was welcomed to Miami alongside Wade, *left*, and Bosh.

Gilbert posted an angry letter on the team's Web site, calling James's decision a "shocking act of disloyalty from our home grown 'chosen one.'"[4]

WELCOME TO MIAMI

Despite the angry backlash, James felt signing with the Heat was the right choice for his career. He didn't believe he could win a championship in Cleveland, where he often had to carry the team on his own. In Miami, James would join superstars Dwyane Wade and Chris Bosh.

The day after *The Decision*, thousands of Heat fans welcomed James at AmericanAirlines Arena.

They cheered as James predicted multiple NBA championships in the Heat's future.

However, fans elsewhere were not so impressed. Even NBA legends such as Jordan and Charles Barkley weighed in with some uncertainty about James's choice.

"There's no way, with hindsight, I would've ever called up Larry [Bird], called up Magic [Johnson] and said, 'Hey, look, let's get together and play on one team.' But . . . things are different. I can't say that's a bad thing. It's an opportunity these kids have today. In all honesty, I was trying to beat those guys."[5]

—MICHAEL JORDAN, REACTING TO JAMES'S DECISION TO PLAY WITH STARS WADE AND BOSH

NO PLACE LIKE HOME

Despite the angry criticism swirling around him, some people still welcomed James back to Akron in August, when he arrived for his annual bike-riding fund-raiser. James donated bikes to 400 children, then hopped on his own bike to lead them on a ride through downtown Akron.[6] James also took out an ad in the *Akron Beacon Journal*, promising, "I will continue to do everything I can for this city."[7]

Even so, James's new place was in Miami. Although he kept his Akron home, he also bought a mansion in Coconut Grove outside Miami. He was ready to begin a new phase in a new city with a new team.

RINGS

More than ever, James had his eyes set on a championship ring. On October 26, 2010, James played his first game with the Heat. The Heat went down 88–80 as the crowd chanted, "Overrated."[8] The Heat was up and down early in the season before finding its rhythm and going on some winning streaks.

On December 2, James played the Cavaliers for the first time since leaving Cleveland. Despite the crowd's boos and chants of "Akron hates you," James scored 38 points in a 118–90 Heat victory.[9]

A championship ring wasn't the only ring James was thinking about, however. At a New Year's Eve party on December 31, 2011, James proposed to Brinson, presenting her with an engagement ring.

Although he had been with Brinson for nine years and they had two children together, James was nervous as he approached the moment to propose. "It felt like before a Finals game," he said.[10] Brinson said yes, and the couple married on September 14, 2013.

COMING SO CLOSE

The Heat finished the season with a 58–24 record to make the play-offs. The Heat cruised past the

NEW NUMBER, NEW START

James had worn the number 23 since high school in honor of Jordan, who had made the number iconic. But as he began his new start with the Miami Heat in 2010, he set the number aside. James said, "Man, there will never be another Michael Jordan. You'll drive yourself crazy trying to be the next Michael Jordan."[11]

James instead chose the number 6. He had worn it while on the US Olympic team. It was also the number of one of his other heroes, basketball legend Julius "Dr. J" Erving. Number 6 also had personal meaning. It stood for his sons' birthdays: LeBron Jr. was born on October 6, and Bryce was born in June, the sixth month.

James was overcome with disappointment after losing to the Mavericks in Game 6 of the 2011 finals.

76ers, the Celtics, and the Bulls. For the second time in his career, James was going to the NBA Finals. He would face the Dallas Mavericks.

The series went back and forth. With the series tied 2–2, James earned a triple-double in Game 5, but the Heat couldn't pull out a win. The Heat again struggled in Game 6, giving the Mavericks the title.

James was crushed, but he later said losing the 2011 finals was the best thing that could have happened to him.

|||||||||

Putting disappointment behind him, James was filled with new drive for the 2011–12 season.

CHAPTER 10

The Heat Is On

|||||||||||||||||||||||||||||||||||||||||||||||||||||||||||||||||||||||||||||||||||||||

The 2011–12 NBA season got off to a late start when a dispute between players and owners led to a lockout. When the season finally opened on Christmas Day, the Heat topped the Mavericks 105 94. It was a strong statement to defeat the team that had defeated them in the previous NBA Finals. The Heat went on to win eight of the first nine games.

Many sportswriters noticed James seemed like a new player. He had spent the summer training with Dambrot, his first high school coach, who made him get back to basics. He had sought out legend Hakeem Olajuwon, who advised him about playing the post, the area under the basket. He also worked with others on ball handling. Focusing on the basics in the off-season paid off. As the season progressed, he was making more than 60 percent of his shots from the field.

In addition, the Heat had reworked the game plan so James could play any position rather than being restricted to small forward. That meant he was free to shoot or to pass—which made him a double threat.

James continued to face boos and taunts from fans at arenas across the country. Even so, the Heat finished the season with a 46–20 record, and James

RENEWED DEDICATION ||||||||||||||||||||||||||||||||||||||||||||||||||||||||

James's renewed dedication to his game in 2012 meant playing through challenges. James even played against the Phoenix Suns while battling the flu. "I've been fortunate to have packed houses every night I go on the floor. I understand they're coming to watch the Suns tomorrow, but they're also coming to watch us and watch me. . . . I don't want them to leave disappointed. . . . So once the lights turn on and the fans come in and the popcorn starts popping, I'll be ready to go," he said.[1]

was named MVP for the third time in his career. Although he was honored to receive the award, he said, "This is not the award I want, ultimately. I want that championship. That's all that matters to me."[2]

||||||||||||||||||||||||||||||||||||||||||||||||||||||||||||

CHAMPION AT LAST

After defeating the New York Knicks, the Indiana Pacers, and the Boston Celtics in the play-offs, James and the Heat faced the Oklahoma City Thunder in the 2012 finals. In a hard-fought series, the Heat clinched the championship in five games. James finally got what he wanted—his first championship ring. He was also named MVP of the play-offs.

Then in the summer of 2012, James became an Olympic champion once again. He led the US men's team to a gold medal in London, England. Rather than racking up his own points, James dished out assists in many games. The win made him only the second player, along with Jordan, to ever earn an NBA championship, the NBA MVP, and an Olympic gold medal in the same year. James's championship achievements in 2012

James had the double joy of winning the NBA championship as well as being named the Finals MVP in 2012.

also helped win back many fans who had turned against him.

REPEAT WINNER

As the 2012–13 season opened, many commentators noticed how James seemed to be having more fun on the court. He seemed relieved of pressure after winning his first championship. In January 2013, James became the youngest player to score 20,000 career points.

From the beginning of February to the end of March, the Heat went on a 27-game winning streak, the second longest in NBA history. The Heat finished the season 66–16, the league's best record. James was again named MVP, becoming one of only five players ever to receive four or more MVP awards.

In the play-offs, the Heat defeated the Milwaukee Bucks, the Chicago Bulls, and the Indiana Pacers before facing the San Antonio Spurs in the finals. Despite a triple-double by James in Game 1, the Spurs won 92–88. The Heat came back with wins in Games 2 and 4, but lost Games 3 and 5. The Spurs now held a 3–2 series lead. James and the Heat had to win Game 6 to stay in

FUN ON THE COURT

With the pressure finally off, James was having fun in the 2012–13 season. Sometimes the fun was contagious. During halftime on January 25, 2013, James watched courtside as 50-year-old Michael Drysch of McHenry, Illinois, lined up for a half-court hook shot. If he made it, he'd win $75,000 for himself and another $75,000 for the Boys and Girls Clubs of America through the LeBron James Family Foundation.[3] Drysch nailed the difficult shot. James jumped up from the bench, ran onto the court, and tackled him in a hug.

the finals—and they did, with a thrilling 103–100 overtime victory.

Game 7 was close from start to finish. In the last minute, James helped the Heat pull ahead for a 95–88 victory. The Heat had won back-to-back championships, and James was honored with his second straight Finals MVP award.

After the game, James marveled at the road he had taken to earn his second championship: "I'm LeBron James, from Akron, Ohio, from the inner city. I'm not even supposed to be here."[4]

|||||||||||||||||||||||||||||||||||||||||||||||||||||||||||||

A BRIGHT FUTURE

After James's 2013 finals victory, some people wondered if he would remain in Miami for the rest of his career. Although many believed James was happy in Miami, others predicted he might one day return to Cleveland. Perhaps he would head for a new team altogether.

No matter where James played, he was determined to work toward his ultimate goal: "I want to be if not the greatest, one of the greatest to ever play this game."[5] Many in the sports world

In 2013, James hoisted the NBA championship trophy and the Finals MVP trophy for the second year in a row.

thought it was a realistic goal. And some even believed he had already achieved it.

||||||||||

TIMELINE

1984

LeBron Raymone James is born in Akron, Ohio, on December 30 to 16-year-old Gloria James.

1996

James begins playing with the Shooting Stars.

2000

As a freshman, James wins the state championship in March with the Saint Vincent-Saint Mary Fighting Irish.

2003

The Cleveland Cavaliers choose James with the first-overall pick in the NBA draft on June 26.

2003

On October 29, James plays his first regular-season game with the Cavaliers.

2004

James is named Rookie of the Year on April 20.

2001

The Fighting Irish win their second straight state championship.

2002

James appears on the cover of *Sports Illustrated* on February 18 as "The Chosen One."

2003

On March 22, the Fighting Irish win a third state championship and are named national champions.

2004

James is part of the US men's basketball team that wins a bronze medal at the Olympics in Athens, Greece.

2004

Savannah Brinson, James's girlfriend, gives birth to the couple's first son, LeBron Jr., on October 6.

2005

On February 20, James plays in his first NBA All-Star game.

TIMELINE

2007

On June 14, James and Brinson's second son, Bryce Maximus, is born.

2008

James and the US men's basketball team win gold at the Olympic Games in Beijing, China.

2009

On May 5, James receives his first MVP award.

2012

James accepts his third career MVP award.

2012

With the Heat, James wins his first NBA championship and is named Finals MVP.

2012

James leads the US men's basketball team to gold at the Olympics in London, England.

2010

On May 2, James is named NBA MVP for the second year in a row.

2010

On July 8, James announces on ESPN that he is leaving Cleveland to play for the Miami Heat.

2011

On December 31, James asks Brinson to marry him.

2013

On May 5, James receives his fourth NBA MVP award.

2013

The Heat win the NBA championship for the second year, and James is again named Finals MVP.

2013

James and Brinson are married on September 14.

GET THE SCOOP

FULL NAME

LeBron Raymone James

DATE OF BIRTH

December 30, 1984

PLACE OF BIRTH

Akron, Ohio

MARRIAGE

Savannah Brinson (September 14, 2013–)

CHILDREN

LeBron James Jr.

Bryce Maximus James

CAREER HIGHLIGHTS

- Led the Saint Vincent-Saint Mary Fighting Irish to three state championships (2000, 2001, 2003) and one national championship (2003) in high school.
- Was featured on the cover of *Sports Illustrated* when he was only a junior in high school (2002).
- Went straight to the NBA after high school and was drafted by the Cleveland Cavaliers as the first-overall pick (2003).

- Won four league MVP awards (2009, 2010, 2012, and 2013).
- Won two NBA championships with the Miami Heat and was named Finals MVP (2012 and 2013).
- Won a bronze medal (2004) and two gold medals (2008 and 2012) with the US men's Olympic basketball team.

PHILANTHROPY

In 2004, James started the LeBron James Family Foundation, which encourages kids to lead a healthy, active lifestyle and focus on their education. He also supports the Boys and Girls Clubs of America.

> **"I want to be if not the greatest, one of the greatest to ever play this game."**
>
> *—LEBRON JAMES*

GLOSSARY

assist—In basketball, to pass the ball to a player who then scores.

camaraderie—A feeling of friendship among the people in a group.

draft—A system used to assign new players to professional sports teams.

driving—In basketball, moving quickly to the basket while dribbling the ball.

endorsement—The act of recommending a product, such as in an ad, often in return for payment.

franchise—A team that is a member of a professional sports league.

lockout—A temporary work stoppage during labor disputes between an employer and a union.

project—A housing development created and funded by the government, usually for low-income families.

rookie—An athlete playing in his or her first year in a professional sport.

slur—An insulting or offensive word or comment.

sweep—To win every game in a series.

triple-double—When a player accumulates ten or more points, assists, or rebounds in a single game.

ADDITIONAL RESOURCES

SELECTED BIBLIOGRAPHY

James, LeBron, and Buzz Bissinger. *LeBron's Dream Team: How Five Friends Made History*. New York: Penguin, 2009. Print.

Jenkins, Lee. "LeBron James." *Sports Illustrated*. 10 Dec. 2012. *Ebsco: MasterFILE Premier*. Web. 25 Aug. 2013.

Morgan, David Lee, Jr. *LeBron James: The Rise of a Star*. Cleveland: Gray, 2003. Print.

Pluto, Terry, and Brian Windhorst. *LeBron James: The Making of an MVP*. Cleveland: Gray, 2009. Print.

FURTHER READINGS

Christopher, Matt. *On the Court with LeBron James*. New York: Little, 2008. Print.

Sharp, Anne Wallace. *LeBron James*. Detroit: Lucent, 2008. Print.

WEB SITES

To learn more about LeBron James, visit ABDO Publishing Company online at **www.abdopublishing.com**. Web sites about LeBron James are featured on our Book Links page. These links are routinely monitored and updated to provide the most current information available.

PLACES TO VISIT

James A. Rhodes Arena
373 Carroll Street, Akron, OH 44325
330-972-6920
http://www.gozips.com/athletics/facilities/JAR#
During James's junior and senior years of high school, most
of Saint Vincent-Saint Mary's home games were held at the
James A. Rhodes Arena at the University of Akron. James
also accepted his second NBA MVP award at the arena. The
arena hosts basketball camps and other events sponsored
by James, including the LeBron James Skills Academy, the
LeBron James King's Academy, and the King James Shooting
Stars Classic.

Naismith Memorial Basketball Hall of Fame
1000 Hall of Fame Avenue, Springfield, MA 01105
877-4HOOPLA
http://www.hoophall.com
LeBron James isn't in the Basketball Hall of Fame—yet.
But many of his idols from basketball history are. Even as a
young player, James studied the history of the sport and its
greats, including Hall of Famers Michael Jordan and Julius
Erving. In addition to basketball history, the hall of fame
features interactive exhibits, skills challenges, basketball
clinics, and shooting contests.

SOURCE NOTES

CHAPTER 1. CHAMPION AT LAST

1. Lee Jenkins. "Promise Keeper." *SI Vault*. Time Inc., 2 July 2012. Web. 25 Aug. 2013.

2. Howard Beck. "LeBron James Leads Heat Past Thunder for NBA Title." *New York Times*. New York Times, 22 June 2012. Web. 25 Aug. 2013.

3. Lee Jenkins. "Promise Keeper." *SI Vault*. Time, 2 July 2012. Web. 25 Aug. 2013.

4. "Onstage Interview with Wade, Bosh, James - July 9, 2010." *NBA.com*. Turner Sports & Entertainment Digital Network, 9 July 2010. Web. 25 Aug. 2013.

5. Adrian Wojnarowski. "LeBron James Carries NBA Championship Crown." *Yahoo!Sports*. Yahoo!, 22 June 2012. Web. 25 Aug. 2013.

6. Howard Beck. "LeBron James Leads Heat Past Thunder for NBA Title." *New York Times*. New York Times, 22 June 2012. Web. 25 Aug. 2013.

7. Lee Jenkins. "Promise Keeper." *SI Vault*. Time Inc., 2 July 2012. Web. 25 Aug. 2013.

CHAPTER 2. TOUGH START

1. LeBron James and Buzz Bissinger. *LeBron's Dream Team: How Five Friends Made History*. New York: Penguin, 2009. Print. 7.

2. Ibid. 9.

3. Ibid. 12.

4. Lew Freedman. *LeBron James: A Biography*. Westport, CT: Greenwood, 2008. Web. 25 Aug. 2013.

5. LeBron James and Buzz Bissinger. *LeBron's Dream Team: How Five Friends Made History*. New York: Penguin, 2009. Print. 12.

6. Ibid. 16.

CHAPTER 3. SHOOTING STAR

1. Reid Cherner. "LeBron Documentary: Q&A with Coach Dru Joyce." *USA Today*. USA Today, 29 Sept. 2009. Web. 25 Aug. 2013.

2. Terry Pluto and Brian Windhorst. *LeBron James: The Making of an MVP*. Cleveland: Gray, 2009. Print. 32.

CHAPTER 4. HIGH SCHOOL DAYS

1. Charles McGrath. "NBA Star, Now Memoirist, on Hometown Court." *New York Times*. New York Times, 4 Sept. 2009. Web. 25 Aug. 2013.

2. LeBron James and Buzz Bissinger. *LeBron's Dream Team: How Five Friends Made History*. New York: Penguin, 2009. Print. 66.

3. Charles McGrath. "NBA Star, Now Memoirist, on Hometown Court." *New York Times*. New York Times, 4 Sept. 2009. Web. 25 Aug. 2013.

4. "Tattoos." *Nike: LeBron*. NikeLeBron.net, 2013. Web. 25 Aug. 2013.

5. Ibid.

6. LeBron James and Buzz Bissinger. *LeBron's Dream Team: How Five Friends Made History*. New York: Penguin, 2009. Print. 79.

7. Terry Pluto. "LeBron James, Once a Lanky Kid, Has Come a Long Way to the NBA." *Akron Beacon Journal*. Akron Beacon Journal, 20 Apr. 2004. Web. 25 Aug. 2013.

8. Matt McMillen. "LeBron James Pays Homage to the Mothers in His Life." *WebMD*. WebMD, 22 Apr. 2010. Web. 25 Aug. 2013.

CHAPTER 5. NATIONAL ATTENTION

1. "LeBron James Talks about Michael Jordan with Oprah Winfrey." *YouTube*. YouTube, 28 Feb. 2013. Web. 25 Aug. 2013.

2. Grant Wahl. "Ahead of His Class." *SI Vault*. Time, Inc., 18 Feb. 2002. Web. 25 Aug. 2013.

3. LeBron James and Buzz Bissinger. *LeBron's Dream Team: How Five Friends Made History*. New York: Penguin, 2009. Print. 139.

4. Grant Wahl and George Dohrmann. "The Continuing 'Education' of LeBron James." *SI Vault*. Time, 13 Jan. 2003. Web. 25 Aug. 2013.

5. LeBron James and Buzz Bissinger. *LeBron's Dream Team: How Five Friends Made History*. New York: Penguin, 2009. Print. 206.

6. Dale Omori. "LeBron Flourishes as a Student in the Disciplined Routine of a Catholic High School: The Making of an MVP." *Cleveland.com*. Northeast Ohio Media Group, 7 Dec. 2009. Web. 25 Aug. 2013.

7. Howard Beck. "NBA Draft Will Close Book on High School Stars." *New York Times*. New York Times, 28 June 2005. Web. 25 Aug. 2013.

8. LeBron James and Buzz Bissinger. *LeBron's Dream Team: How Five Friends Made History*. New York: Penguin, 2009. Print. 189.

9. Associated Press. "Grounded." *SI.com*. Time, 31 Jan. 2003. Web. 25 Aug. 2013.

10. Seth Stevenson. "Heir Jordan." *Slate*. Slate, 22 May 2003. Web. 25 Aug. 2013.

CHAPTER 6. NBA BOUND

1. "LeBron James: A King's Career." *New York Times*. New York Times, 8 July 2010. Web. 25 Aug. 2013.

2. Terry Pluto and Brian Windhorst. *LeBron James: The Making of an MVP*. Cleveland: Gray, 2009. Print. 79.

3. Dale Omori. "LeBron Enters the NBA with Comparisons to the 'Blessed Trinity' of Magic, Bird and Jordan: The Making of an MVP." *Cleveland.com*. Northeast Ohio Media Group, 8 Dec. 2009. Web. 25 Aug. 2013.

4. "LeBron James Impresses World." *InsideHoops.com*. InsideHoops.com, 30 Oct. 2003. Web. 25 Aug. 2013.

5. Tom Withers. "Childhood Experiences Shape Cavs' James." *AP Online*. 11 Dec. 2005. *Ebsco: Newspaper Source Plus*. Web. 25 June 2013.

6. Associated Press. "AP Interview: LeBron James Beyond His Years, Beyond the Hype." *ESPN.com*. ESPN Internet Ventures, 10 Dec. 2005. Web. 25 Aug. 2013.

7. "Our Mission." *The LeBron James Family Foundation*. The LeBron James Family Foundation, 2013. Web. 25 Aug. 2013.

8. Brian Windhorst. "Charting LeBron's Evolution, Debut by Debut." *ESPN.com*. ESPN Internet Ventures, 27 Apr. 2006. Web. 25 Aug. 2013.

CHAPTER 7. FALLING SHORT

1. Terry Pluto and Brian Windhorst. *The Franchise: LeBron James and the Remaking of the Cleveland Cavaliers*. Cleveland: Gray, 2007. Print. 193.

2. Ibid. 197.

3. "NBA Finals: Cavaliers v Spurs." *ASAP Sports*. ASAP Sports, 14 June 2007. Web. 25 Aug. 2013.

4. Tom Withers. "Childhood Experiences Shape Cavs' James." *AP Online*. 11 Dec. 2005. *Ebsco: Newspaper Source Plus*. Web. 25 June 2013.

5. "A Look into LeBron James' Personal Life." *YouTube*. YouTube, 7 May 2008. Web. 25 Aug. 2013.

6. Ibid.

CHAPTER 8. MOST VALUABLE PLAYER

1. Pete Thamel. "Among the Stars, James Seems to Shine a Bit Brighter." *New York Times*. New York Times, 20 Aug. 2008. Web. 25 Aug. 2013.

2. Jeff Zillgitt. "King James Seeking True Royalty: First Crown for Cavs." *USA Today*. USA Today, 28 Oct. 2008. Web. 25 Aug. 2013.

3. Roger Moore. "LeBron James Grows Up in Front of the Cameras in *More Than a Game*." *Orlando Sentinel*. Tribune Newspaper Company, 5 Oct. 2009. Web. 25 Aug. 2013.

4. Terry Pluto and Brian Windhorst. *LeBron James: The Making of an MVP*. Cleveland: Gray, 2009. Print. 9.

5. William C. Rhoden. "A Handshake Is Not Too Much to Ask, Even from a King." *New York Times*. New York Times, 1 June 2009. Web. 25 Aug. 2013.

6. Sean D. Hamill. "For James, Game-Day Quirks Evolve into the Ritual." *New York Times*. New York Times, 11 Feb. 2010. Web. 25 Aug. 2013.

CHAPTER 9. *THE DECISION*

1. Howard Beck. "NBA's Season of Suspense Ends." *New York Times*. New York Times, 8 July 2010. Web. 25 Aug. 2013.

2. Ian Thomsen. "The Plot Starts Here . . . Showtime Starts Here." *SI Vault*. Time, Inc., 19 July 2010. Web. 25 Aug. 2013.

3. Ibid.

4. Sean Gregory. "A Sad, Strange Night for LeBron James." *Time*. Time, 9 July 2010. Web. 25 Aug. 2013.

5. "Jordan Wouldn't Have Called Magic, Bird." *ESPN.com*. ESPN Internet Ventures, 19 July 2010. Web. 25 Aug. 2013.

6. Christopher Maag. "Back in His Hometown, James Remains Royalty, Whatever His Uniform." *New York Times*. New York Times, 7 Aug. 2010. Web. 25 Aug. 2013.

7. Ibid.

8. Associated Press. "Despite 31 Points from LeBron James, the Miami Heat Fizzle against the Boston Celtics, 88–80." *Cleveland.com*. Northeast Ohio Media Group, 27 Oct. 2010. Web. 25 Aug. 2013.

9. Sean Gregory. "Miss Me? LeBron James Torches Cleveland." *Time.com*. Time, 3 Dec. 2010. Web. 29 June 2013.

10. "How LeBron James Proposed to His Sweetheart—Oprah's Next Chapter." *YouTube*. YouTube, 2 July 2012. Web. 25 Aug. 2013.

11. Chris Broussard. "Air Standards Seem out of Reach." *ESPN.com*. ESPN Internet Ventures, 28 May 2009. Web. 25 Aug. 2013.

CHAPTER 10. THE HEAT IS ON

1. Lee Jenkins. "Promise Keeper." *SI Vault*. Time, 2 July 2012. Web. 25 Aug. 2013.

2. Associated Press. "James Talks of Titles, Not M.V.P." *New York Times*. New York Times, 12 May 2012. Web. 25 Aug. 2013.

3. Harvey Araton. "Lessons from a Hug by LeBron James." *New York Times*. New York Times, 30 Jan. 2013. Web. 25 Aug. 2013.

4. Howard Beck. "Pushed to Limit, James and Miami Repeat as NBA Champions." *New York Times*. New York Times, 20 June 2013. Web. 25 Aug. 2013.

5. Al Iannazzone. "LeBron James Again Answers His Critics." *Newsday*. 21 June 2013. *Ebsco: Newspaper Source Plus*. Web. 25 June 2013.

INDEX

ABOUT THE AUTHOR

Valerie Bodden is a freelance author and editor. She has written more than 100 children's nonfiction books. Her books have received positive reviews from *School Library Journal*, *Booklist*, *Children's Literature*, *ForeWord Magazine*, *Horn Book Guide*, *VOYA*, and *Library Media Connection*. Bodden lives in Wisconsin with her husband and four children.